HAL LEONARD DULCIMER SERIES

T0039465

HITS OF THE BEATLES
By Neal Hellman

*With special guest arrangements by:
Lorraine Lee, Leo Kretzner, Steve Isom,
Phyllis Dunne and Shelley Stevens.*

Contents

All arrangements by Neal J. Hellman except where noted.

Special thanks to Joe Weed, Marti Kendell, Joy Cooper-Van Auken, Azalea Nash, Shiloh Hellman, Cathy Lenox and Steve Isom.

Dedicated to Stuart Sutcliffe and, of course, The Beatles.

*This publication contains songs made famous by The Beatles.
The Beatles are not connected in any way with Northern Songs or its licensees.*

HAL•LEONARD CORPORATION

7777 W. BLUEMOUND RD. P.O. BOX 13819 MILWAUKEE, WI 53213

ABOUT THE AUTHOR

Neal Hellman is an internationally known performer on the dulcimer appearing in concerts and festivals throughout North America and Europe. He has authored numerous books for dulcimer including **The Dulcimer Chord Book, Dulcimer Airs, Ballads and Bears, Appalachian Dulcimer Duets, The Pacific Rim Dulcimer Book** and several others. Neal's recordings include **Dulcimer Airs, Ballads and Bears, Appalachian Dulcimer Duets, A Dulcimer Christmas,** the **Pacific Rim Dulcimer Project** and **Oktober County.**

INTRODUCTION

It's very interesting how we can remember where we were and what we were doing on the day of an important historical or social event. Most post-war baby boomers can remember what they were doing when the first man landed on the Moon or the day Kennedy was shot. I can vividly remember walking down east 27th street in Brooklyn and hearing, "I Want to Hold Your Hand" blaring out of Tony del Franco's AM radio in his blue and white '56 chevy. "Hey Tony," I said, "turn it up!" I somehow knew that the entire face of popular music would never be the same.

Though the years between 1965-1971 were turbulent and full of changes, I feel both fortunate and wiser for having been part of that generation. The Beatles were the sound track for this period of time, matching it both in its intense joy and pain.

Arranging their music for the dulcimer has let me relive those years to an extent. I can say in all honesty it has been a true joy creating this work.

I would like to especially thank Todd Lowry for his advice on arranging, Will Schmid for creating the idea for the book and Lorraine, Leo, Shelley, Phyllis and Steve for their very special arrangements.

Neal J. Hellman
Spring 1987

UNDERSTANDING THE TABLATURE

The system used here is essentially the same I have used in my other books. Here's a quick review before you start.

HEY JUDE

Words and Music by JOHN LENNON
and PAUL McCARTNEY

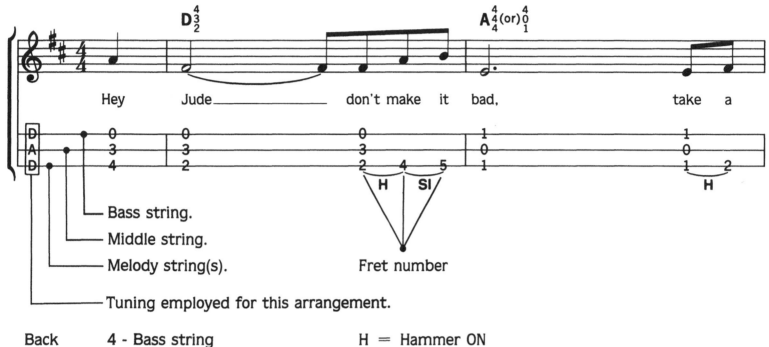

Back	4 - Bass string	H = Hammer ON
up	3 - Middle string	SL = Slide
Chords	2 - Melody string (s)	P = Pull OFF.

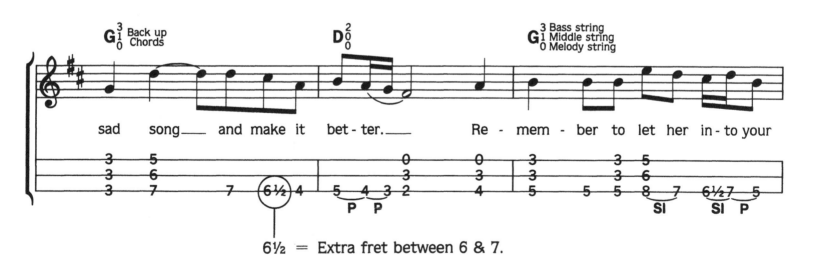

6½ = Extra fret between 6 & 7.

Play what you see! ———— means play just the 7th fret of the melody string.
7

Note: Both Lorraine Lee's tablature (Here Comes The Sun) and Leo Kretzner's (All My Lovin') are slightly different than mine. Please consult "Playing Tips For Each Tune" section before playing the pieces. The same is true for the arrangements by Phyllis Dunne (Michelle) and Shelly Stevens (Yesterday).

PLAYING TIPS FOR EACH ARRANGEMENT

Think of each arrangement as a recipe. We all know how to alter something out of a cookbook to suit our own taste. Please feel free to do the same here. An arrangement is like a photograph; it freezes something that is in motion that is never really the same twice. If you would rather just play the melody note instead of the full chord, by all means do so. Perhaps you'd rather not use a certain slide or pull-off as I do. Please tailor these arrangements to your own style of playing. Try experimenting with different sets of "back-up" chords as well. Check the enclosed charts for additional chords.

All My Loving: Arr. Leo Kretzner
Note: the melody (for the dulcimer) is written literally as in the standard notation (i.e., as the vocal was sung). This necessitates syncopated chord changes if the dulcimer plays a chord melody arrangement, as here. Alternatively, dulcimer chord changes could come on the down beat (as in standard notation) and the rhythm of the melody changed slightly.

Also: The chord of each measure is written once at the beginning of the measure, but in fact, I try to hold it down and strum it along with the melody throughout the measure.

All Together Now: This is arranged for back-up dulcimer. To emulate the "chucka-chucka" rhythm on the record (Yellow Submarine), try dampening the strings between beats by strumming without pushing down all the way to sound the notes.

And I Love Her: I'm partial to the back-up chords and just singing this early Beatles' composition. Though I do enjoy the lead or melody arrangement, I love to play the back-up chords with that kind of 50's flamenco strum. Here are two methods to employ this effect:

1) Utilizing your hand: Strum across all the strings with your index finger. Now follow in rapid succession with your index, middle and ring fingers. Now return with an up strum (toward yourself) with your index finger, followed by three quick down strums with the same finger. Keep repeating the process, and soon you'll be a master of the funky 50's flamenco strum.

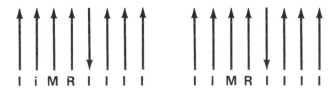

2) Using a flatpick: Strum away from you and on the up strum be sure to articulate each string, then a down strum followed by three quick down strums.

Eleanor Rigby: The embellishments are essential to this composition. It just wouldn't have the macabre feel to it without all the hammers and pulls. **Note:** Dulcimer tuned-C-A-D.

Golden Slumbers: This is a lullaby, so play it slow and gentle. Remember you can change the embellishments, or drop some, or add a few of your own.

Here Comes The Sun: Here Comes the Sun has cheered me on and been a song of comfort and celebration to me for years. When Neal invited me to contribute an arrangement for his book it was my first choice. Of course, George Harrison did not write this song using a dulcimer. To play it with accuracy your dulcimer will need an "**extra**" (6 1/2) **and a capo.** Further, the timing is syncopated and complex. My guess is that most of you already know and love this song. Consider my tab as a guide to help with fingerings, and you'll quickly be playing it.

To play my tablature accurately, here is the key to my rhythm notation: fret numbers with connected stems (⊔) have the time value of half a beat each. Unconnected numbers have the time value of a full beat. A dash extends a note for an additional beat. Curved lines (ties) indicate that the string is not struck again to sound the tied note. Rather, sustain the note just sounded for the additional length of the tied note.

Guitarist Bennett Hammond suggests that **Here Comes the Sun** is "A future traditional tune from the British Isles". I agree. Enjoy this beautiful song and shape your own arrangement.

Lorraine Lee, Brookline, Mass., June 1987

Hey Jude: If all the big chords are too much for your taste try just playing the melody note. You can find the note by looking at the musical staff directly above the chord in question. For example, instead of playing the $\frac{4}{2}$ just pick the 2 to sound the correct melody note.

I Feel Fine: The embellishments on line three bar 3 and line 7 bar 3 are fundamental to the arrangement.

I Will: Start with the back-up chords. Get into the "lilt" of the song. When you feel comfortable, try the melody line. Play the melody very, very slowly 'till you feel confident with the piece. Increase the tempo little by little 'till you get it up to the speed on the record.

It's All Too Much: Remember to tune D-G-D for this one. You can just play the melody on the first string with the others open if you wish.

It's Only Love: Similar form used in **And I Love Her.** Learn the back-up part first. Get comfortable with the rhythm of the piece before attempting the melody part.

Let It Be: This arrangement is a lot easier than it appears to be. Remember to articulate each full chord, sometimes soft and sometimes loud. Put your feelings in your playing.

Michelle: This fingerpicking arrangement is tuned CC-F#-D. You can find the F# by playing the second fret of the bass string. C can be found on the sixth fret of the bass string.   Arr. Phyllis Dunne.

The back-up chords are to be played on a different dulcimer tuned DD-A-D.

Norwegian Wood (This Bird Has Flown): Note: the $\frac{4}{2}_{1}$ in line one bar 3. If you do not want to play the entire chord just hammer or strike the 2nd fret middle string. One can place greater attention on the melody by picking just melody notes instead of the entire chord.

Nowhere Man: To make it easier, retune the dulcimer to D-G-D and play just the melody line. You could also capo on the 3rd fret and play the melody line.   Arr. Steve Isom.

Ob-La-Di, Ob-La-Da: Tune D-G-D. The entire melody can be played on the first string(s). This is a fun song. Be sure and keep the enthusiastic strum energy up.

Rain: Another in D-G-D. Once again the melody can be played on only the first string(s) if you wish.

She's Leaving Home: For two dulcimers. Please note how the two dulcimers seem to switch places on the tab. The second part can be played by another instrument as long as it plays the back-up chords and the melody line laid out for it.

Tell Me What You See: A gentle fingerpicking style would suit this sweet little love ballad very well.

Yellow Submarine: Once again, here you can eliminate some of the chords by playing the melody on the first string(s). Keep it bouncy, and fun.

Yesterday: Written for 4-equidistant strings. Instructions given with tune. Arr. Shelly Stevens.

You've Got To Hide Your Love Away: Keep the rhythm chords even. I know you'll have to stretch for some, but it's well worth the effort. Arranged for back-up only. If some of the chords are too difficult, consult the chart (p. 62) for ones that are simpler. Try using $\frac{4}{0}_{1}$ for an (A) chord instead of $\frac{4}{2}_{1}$.

You've Got to Hide Your Love Away

Words and Music by JOHN LENNON
and PAUL McCARTNEY

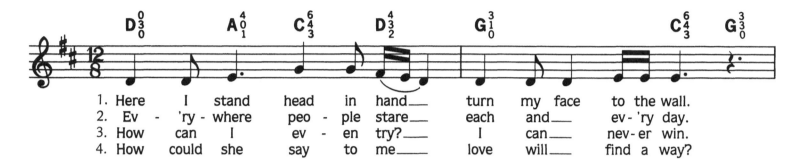

1. Here I stand head in hand___ turn my face to the wall.
2. Ev - 'ry - where peo - ple stare___ each and___ ev - 'ry day.
3. How can I ev - en try?___ I can___ nev - er win.
4. How could she say to me___ love will___ find a way?

If she's gone I can't go on___ feel - ing two foot small.___
I can see them laugh at me___ and I hear them say,___
Hear - ing them, see - ing them___ in the state I'm in.___
Ga - ther round all you clowns,___ let me hear you say,___

Hey you've_got to hide your_ love a -

Hey you've_got to hide your_ love a - way.___

AND I LOVE HER

Words and Music by JOHN LENNON
and PAUL McCARTNEY

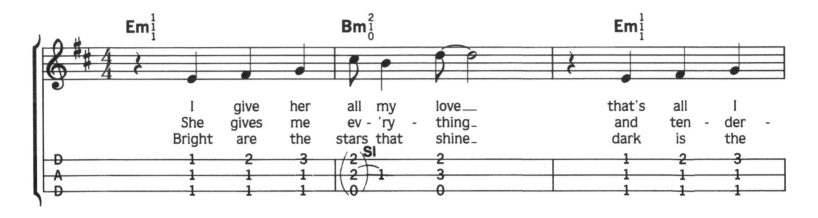

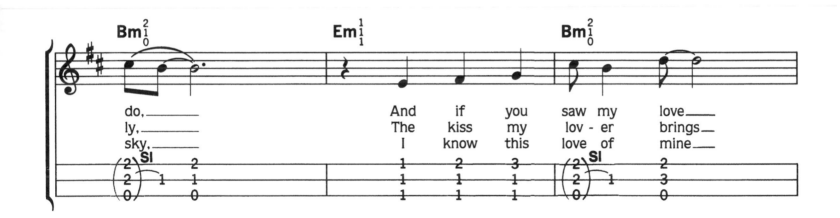

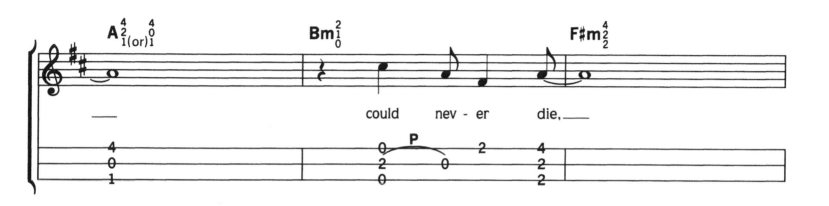

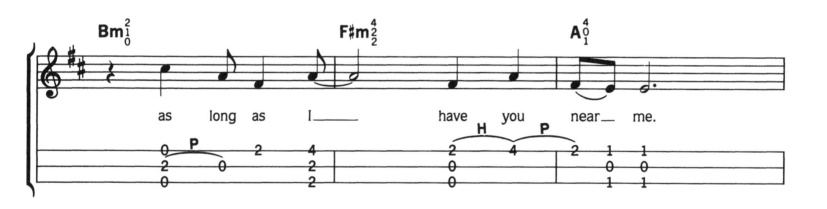

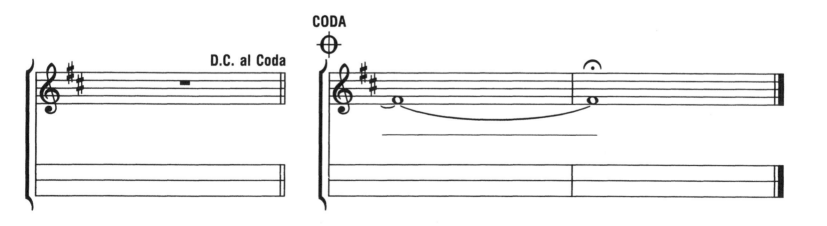

9

NOWHERE MAN

Words and Music by JOHN LENNON
and PAUL McCARTNEY

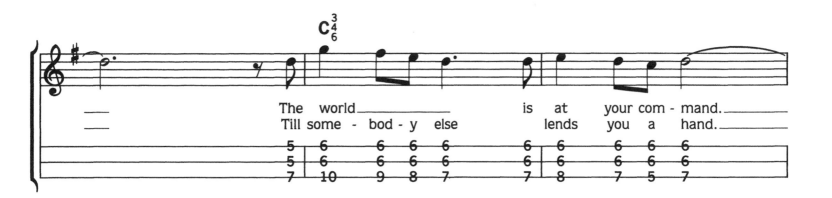

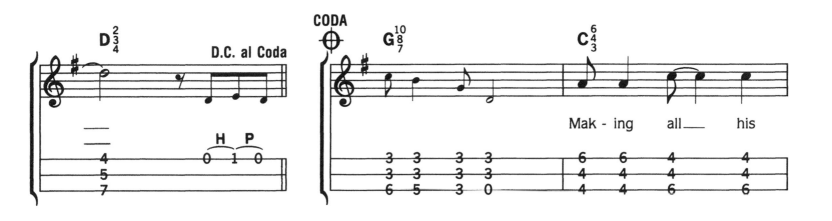

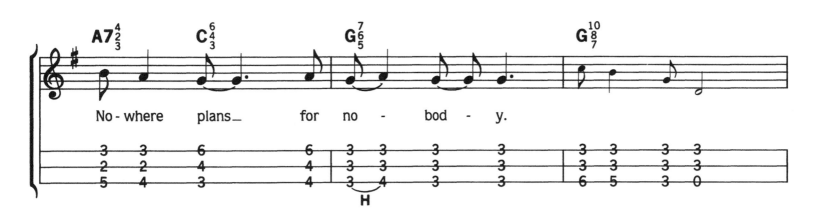

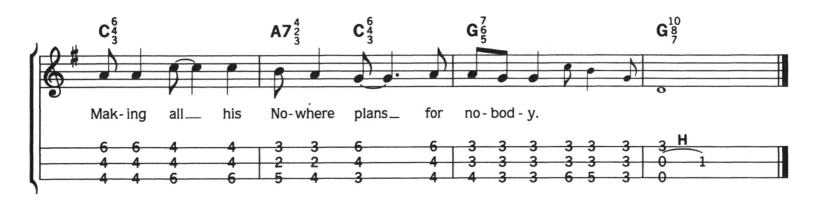

NORWEGIAN WOOD
(This Bird Has Flown)

Words and Music by JOHN LENNON
and PAUL McCARTNEY

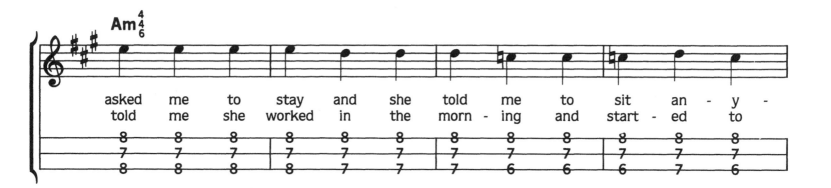

asked me to stay and she told me to sit an - y -
told me she worked in the morn - ing and start - ed to

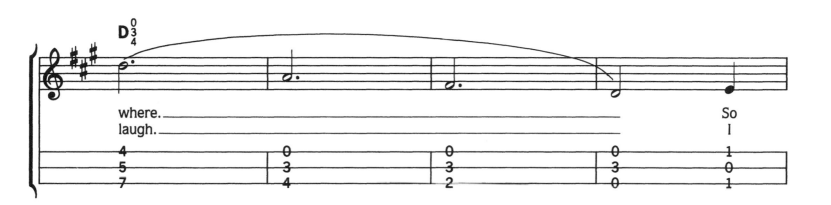

where. _____ So
laugh. _____ I

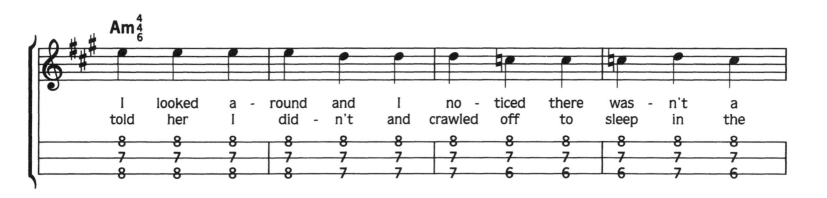

I looked a - round and I no - ticed there was - n't a
told her I did - n't and crawled off to sleep in the

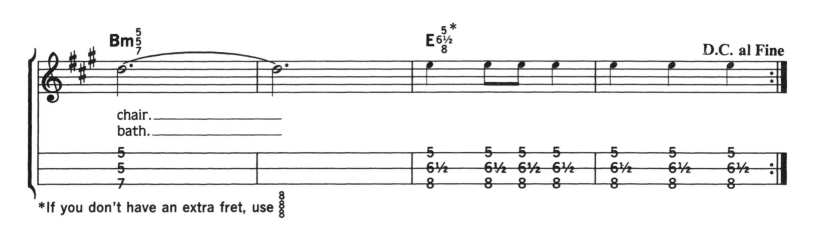

chair. _____
bath. _____

D.C. al Fine

*If you don't have an extra fret, use $\frac{8}{8}$

13

LET IT BE

Words and Music by JOHN LENNON
and PAUL McCARTNEY

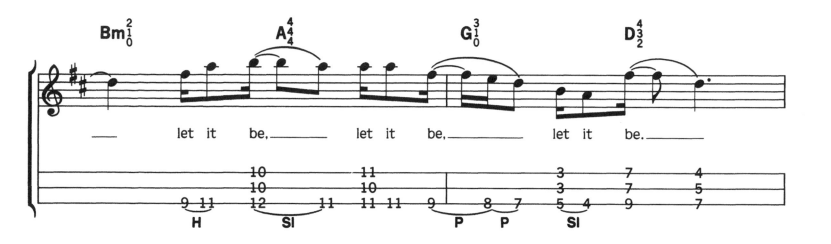

let it be,_____ let it be,_____ let it be.

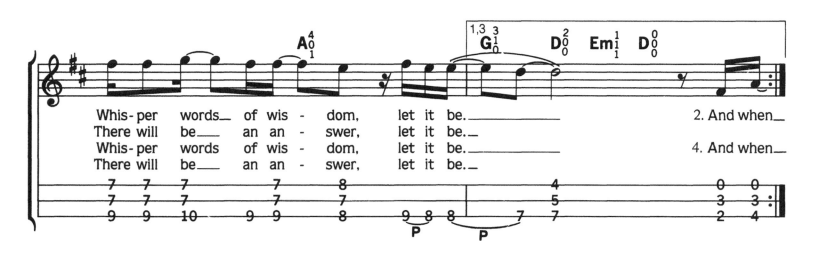

Whis-per words___ of wis - dom, let it be._____ 2. And when___
There will be___ an an - swer, let it be._
Whis-per words of wis - dom, let it be._____ 4. And when___
There will be___ an an - swer, let it be._

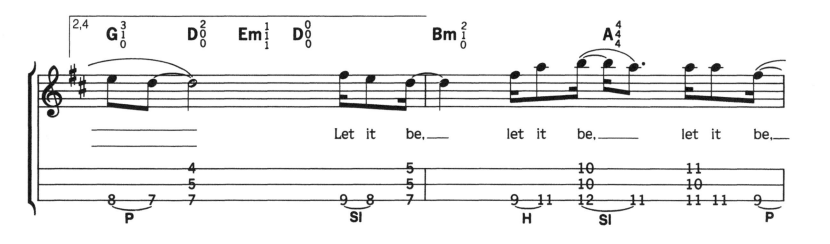

_____ Let it be,___ let it be,_____ let it be,___

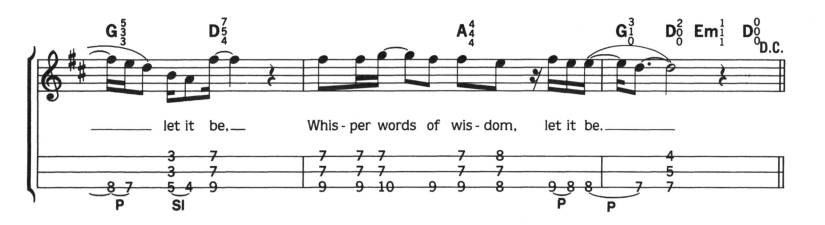

___ let it be,___ Whis - per words of wis - dom, let it be._____

ALL MY LOVING

Words and Music by JOHN LENNON
and PAUL McCARTNEY

17

ELEANOR RIGBY

Words and Music by JOHN LENNON
and PAUL McCARTNEY

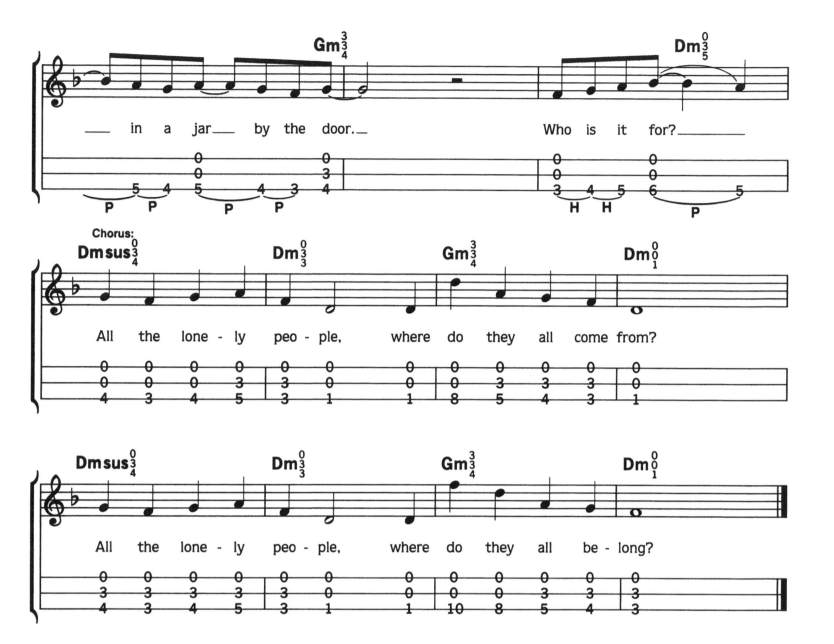

Additional lyrics

2. Father McKenzie, writing the words of a sermon that no one will hear, no one comes near.
   Look at him working, darning his socks in the night when there's nobody there, what does he care?
   All the lonely people, where do they all come from?
   All the lonely people, where do they all belong? (Chorus)

3. Eleanor Rigby, died in the church and was buried along with her name, nobody came.
   Father McKenzie, wiping the dirt from his hands as he walks from the grave, no one was saved.
   All the lonely people, where do they all come from?
   All the lonely people, where do they all belong? (Chorus)

ALL TOGETHER NOW

Words and Music by JOHN LENNON
and PAUL McCARTNEY

G D7
One, two, three, four, Can I have a lit - tle more.
G D7 G
Five, six, sev - en, eight, nine, ten, I love you.
D7
A, B, C, D, Can I bring my friend to tea?
G D7 G
E, F, G, H, I, J, I love you.
G G G C G
(Bom Bom Bom Bom - pa Bom) Sail the ship (Bom - pa Bom)
C D
Chop the tree (Bom - pa Bom) Skip the rope (Bom - pa Bom)
D7 To Coda G
Look at me (All to - geth - er now) All to - geth - er
G D7
now (All to - geth - er now) All to - geth - er now (All to - geth - er now) All to - geth - er

GOLDEN SLUMBERS

Words and Music by JOHN LENNON
and PAUL McCARTNEY

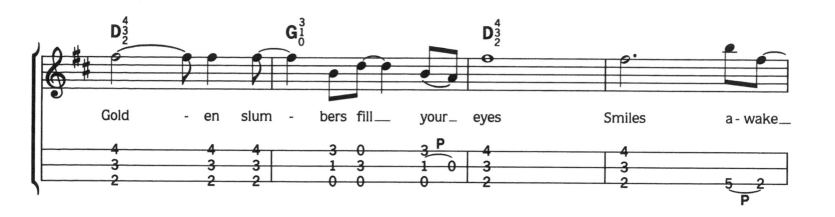

Gold - en slum - bers fill___ your___ eyes   Smiles   a-wake___

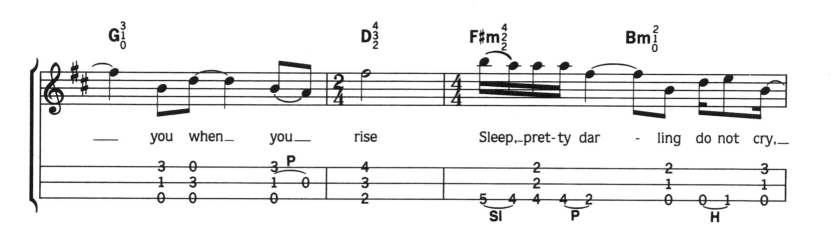

___ you when___ you___ rise   Sleep,__pret-ty dar - ling do not cry,___

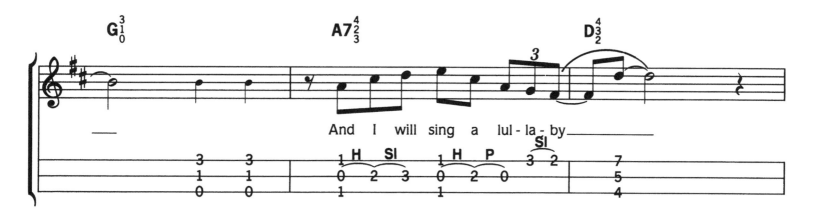

And   I   will   sing   a   lul - la - by_____

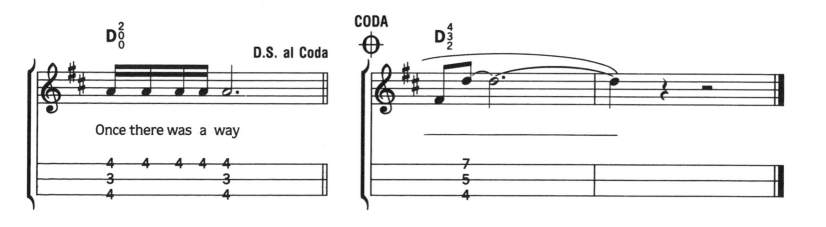

Once there was a way

I FEEL FINE

Words and Music by JOHN LENNON
and PAUL McCARTNEY

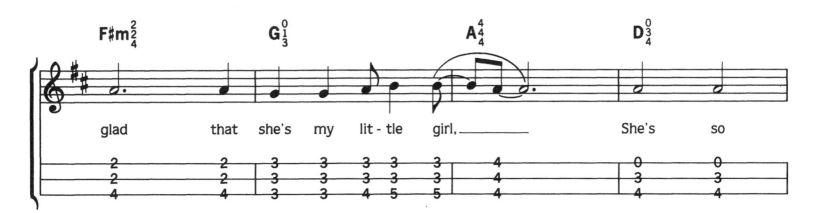

glad that she's my lit - tle girl, _____ She's so

glad she's tell - ing all the world, __ that her ba -

D.C. al Coda

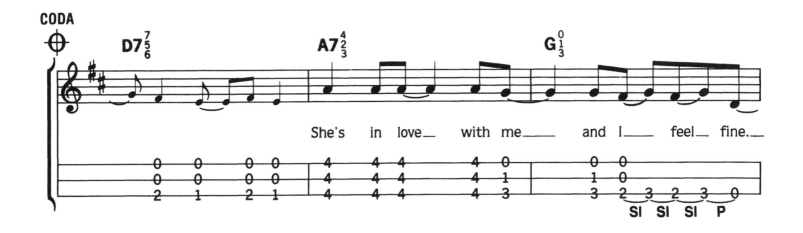

She's in love__ with me____ and I____ feel__ fine.__

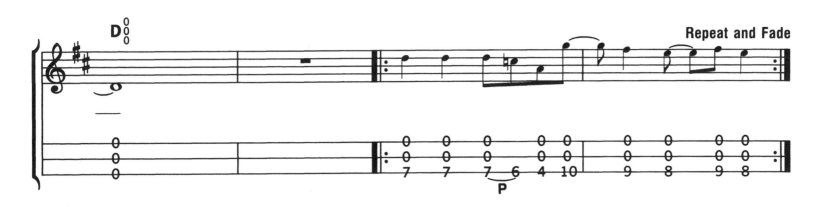

Repeat and Fade

IT'S ALL TOO MUCH

Words and Music by
GEORGE HARRISON

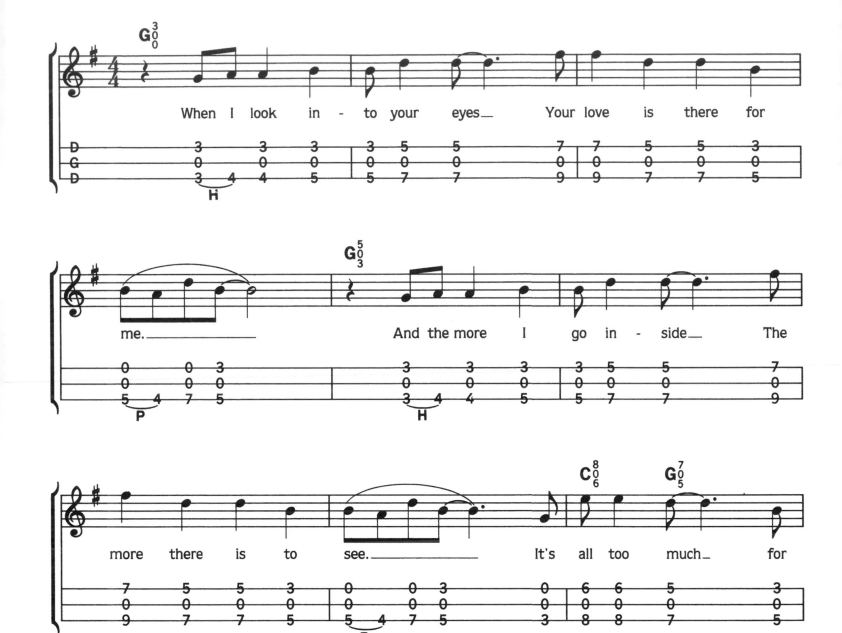

When I look in - to your eyes___ Your love is there for
me._____ And the more I go in - side___ The
more there is to see._____ It's all too much___ for

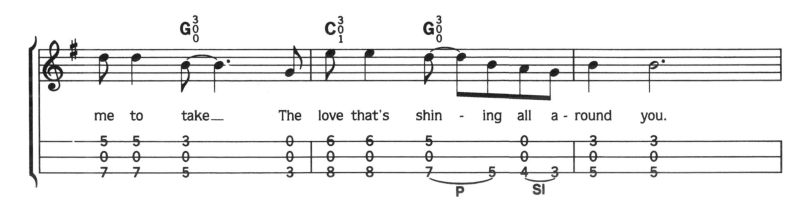

me to take___ The love that's shin - ing all a - round you.

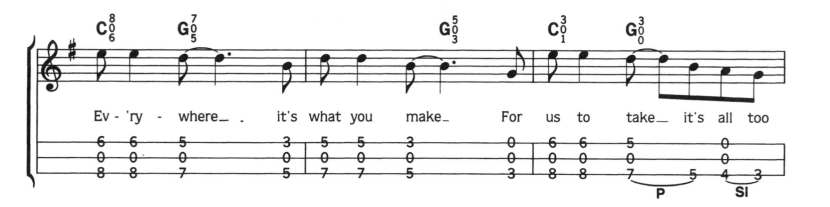

Ev - 'ry - where_ . it's what you make_ For us to take_ it's all too

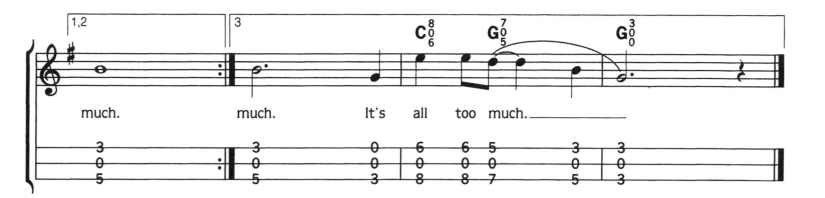

much. much. It's all too much.___

Additional lyrics

2. Floating down the stream of time
   From life to life with me.
   Makes no difference where you are
   Or where you'd like to be.
   It's all too much for me to take
   The love that's shining all around you.
   All the world is birthday cake
   So take a piece but not too much.

3. Sail me on a silver sun,
   Where I know that I'm free.
   Show me that I'm everywhere
   And get me home for tea.
   It's all too much for me to take
   There's plenty there for everybody.
   The more you give the more you get
   The more it is and it's too much.

IT'S ONLY LOVE

Words and Music by JOHN LENNON
and PAUL McCARTNEY

28

RAIN

Words and Music by JOHN LENNON
and PAUL McCARTNEY

31

TELL ME WHAT YOU SEE

Words and Music by JOHN LENNON
and PAUL McCARTNEY

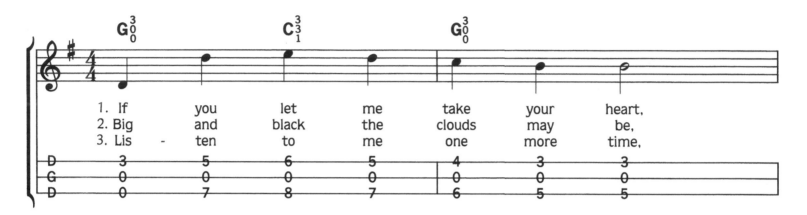

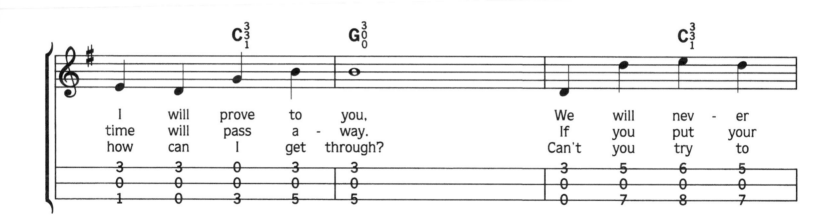

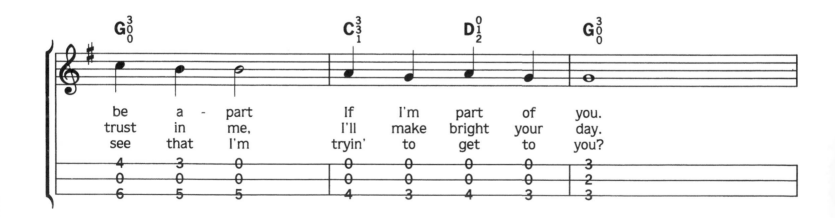

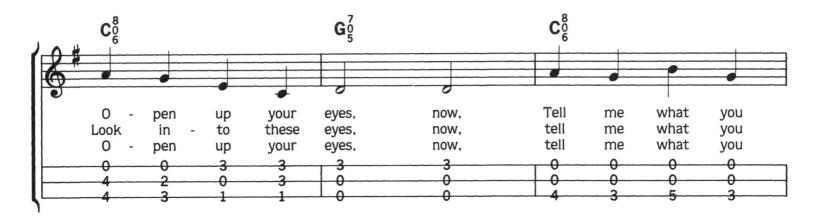

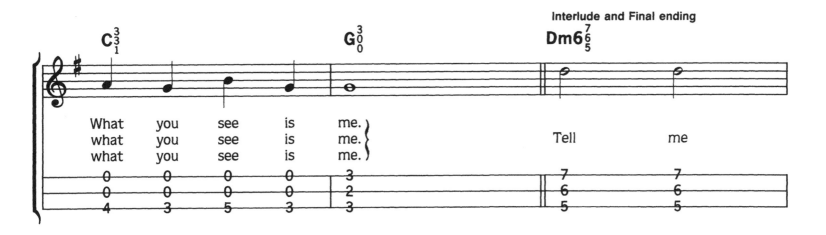

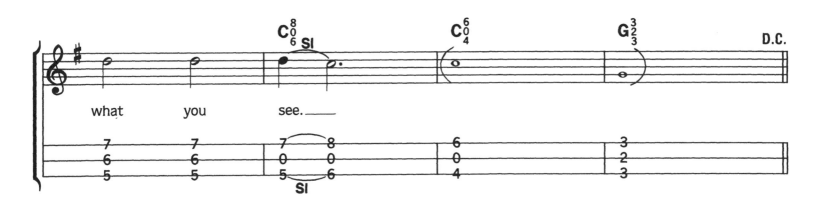

33

HEY JUDE

Words and Music by JOHN LENNON
and PAUL McCARTNEY

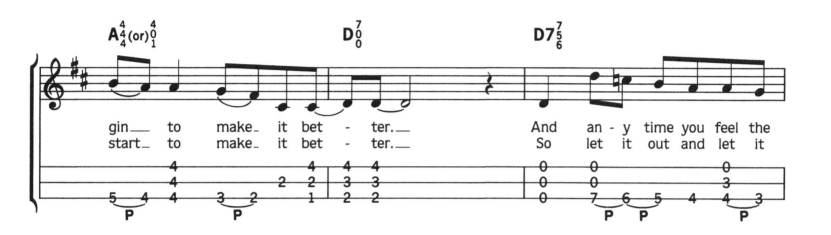

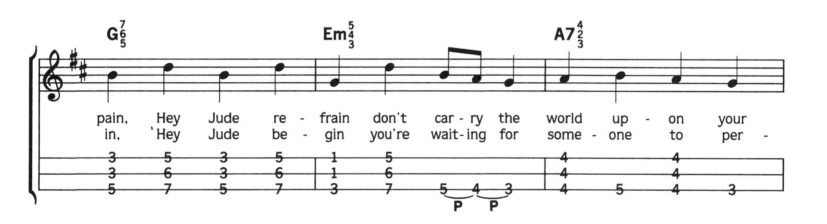

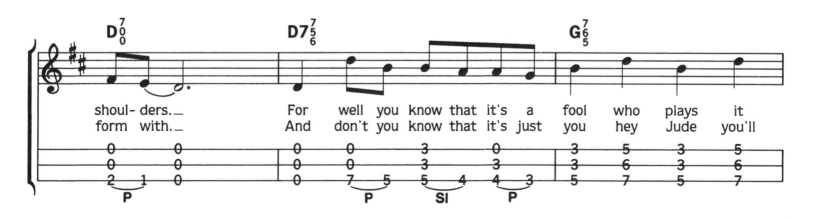

35

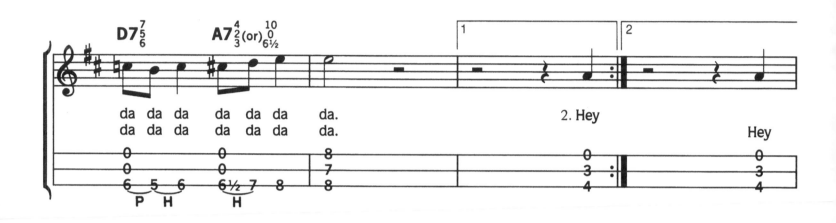

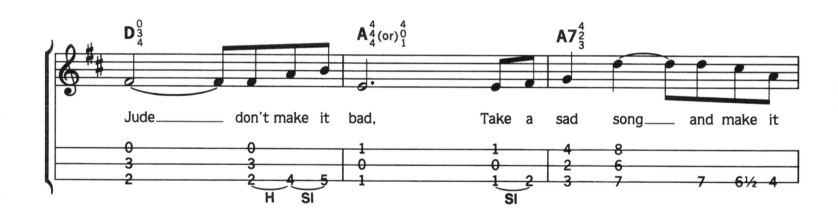

36

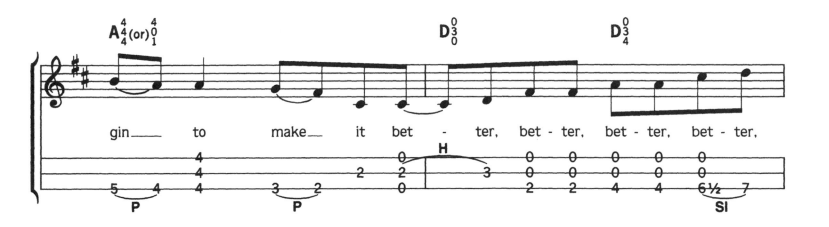

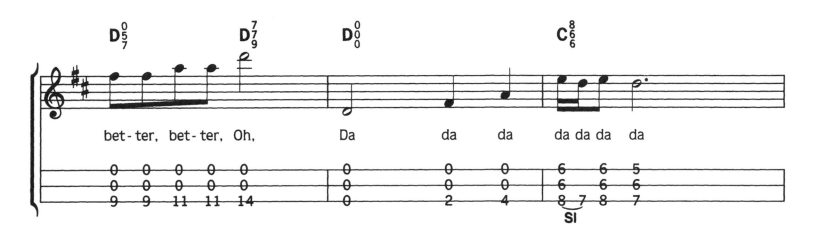

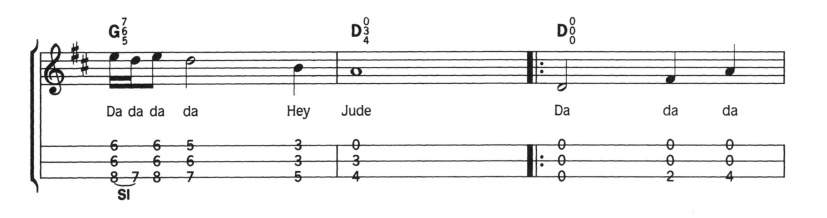

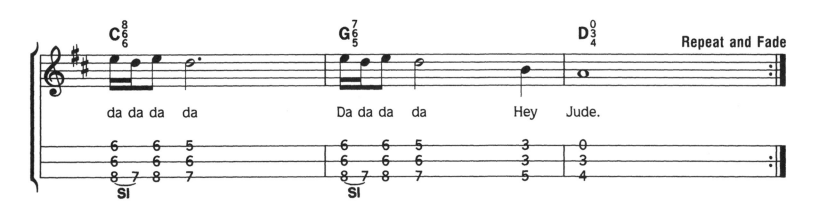

OB-LA-DI, OB-LA-DA

Words and Music by JOHN LENNON
and PAUL McCARTNEY

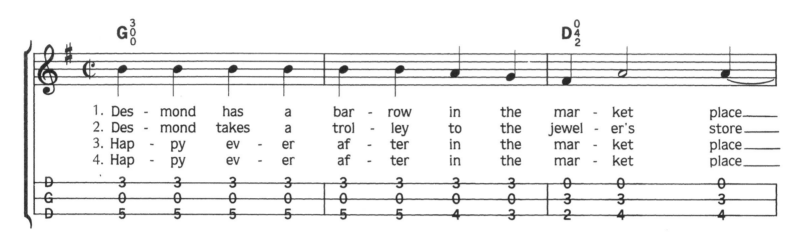

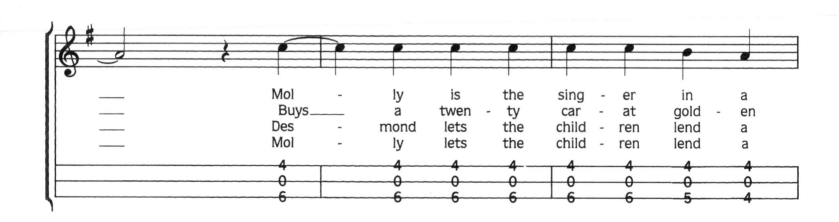

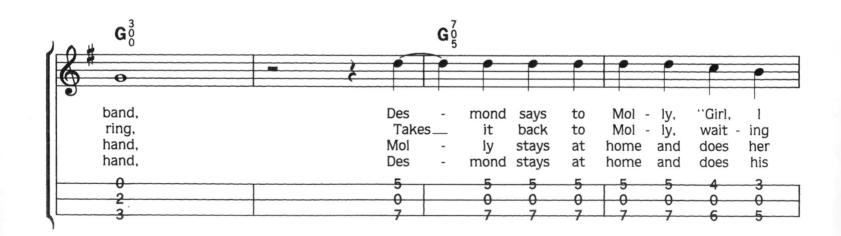

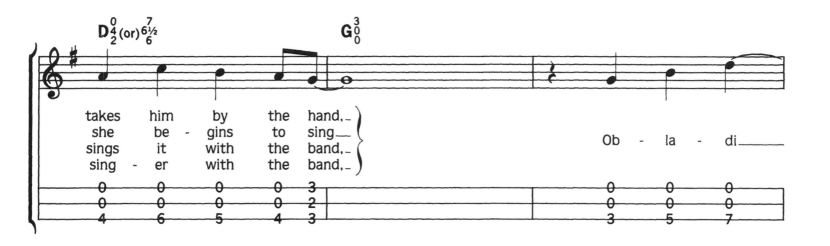

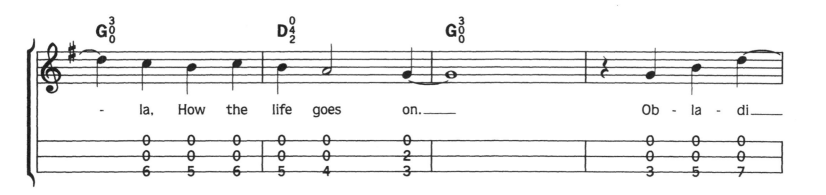

39

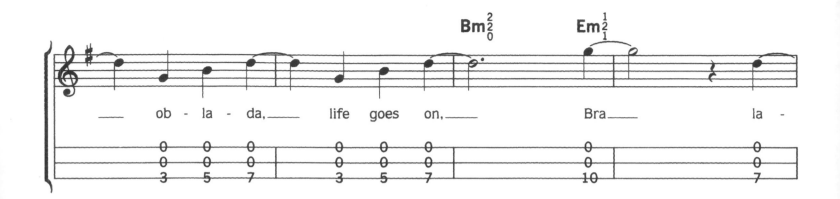

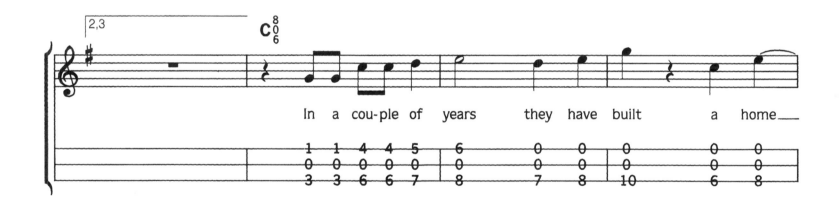

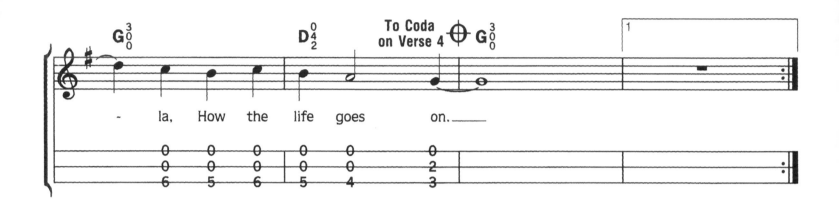

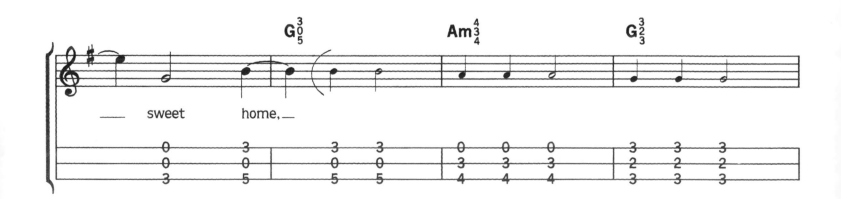

40

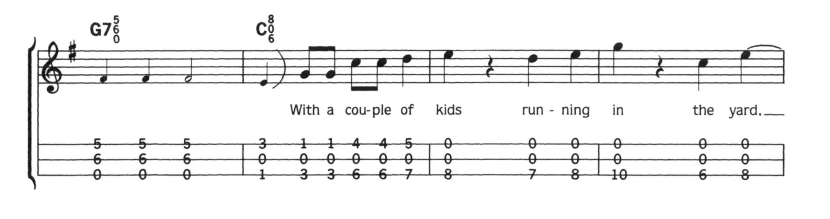

With a cou-ple of kids run-ning in the yard,___

___ Of Des - mond and Mol — ly Jones.___

D.C.
Take Coda
on Verse 4

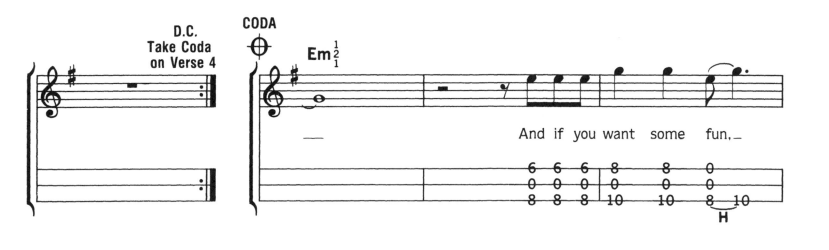

CODA

And if you want some fun,___

H

Take Ob - la - di - bla - da.

I WILL

Words and Music by JOHN LENNON
and PAUL McCARTNEY

YELLOW SUBMARINE

Words and Music by JOHN LENNON
and PAUL McCARTNEY

46

SHE'S LEAVING HOME

YESTERDAY

If your dulcimer is not set up with 4 equidistant strings you can play chordal background to this tune on 3 strings — tune D-A-D. To play melody you need 4 equidistant strings and a 6½ fret. Tune D-A#-A-D (low to high). This is a chromatic tuning I learned from Janita Baker. Once you get the knack of fingerpicking each string separately, this tuning opens up a whole new world on the dulcimer.

Words and Music by JOHN LENNON
and PAUL McCARTNEY

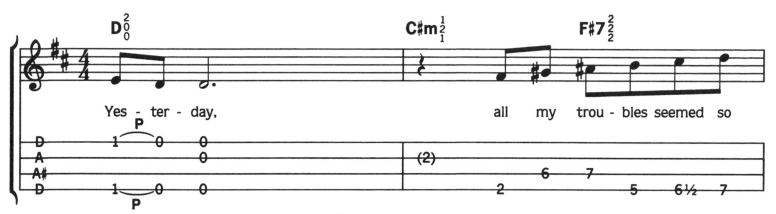

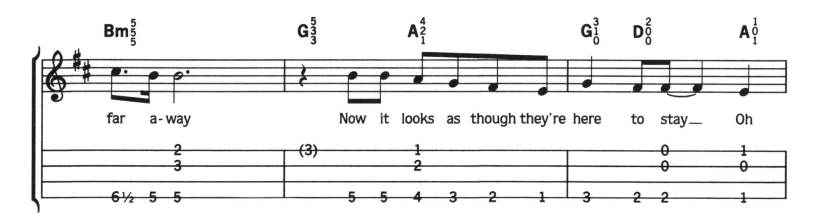

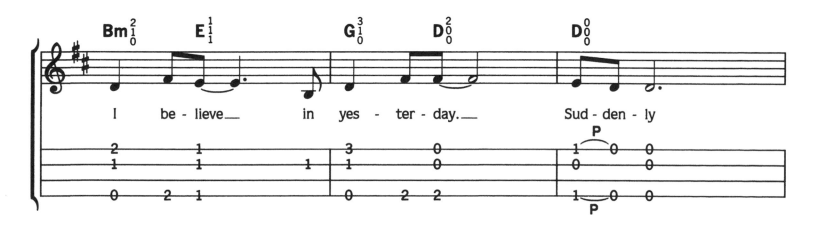

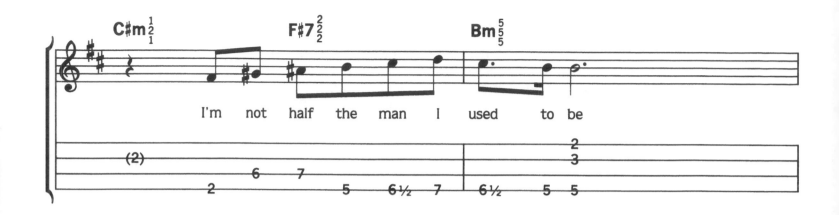

I'm not half the man I used to be

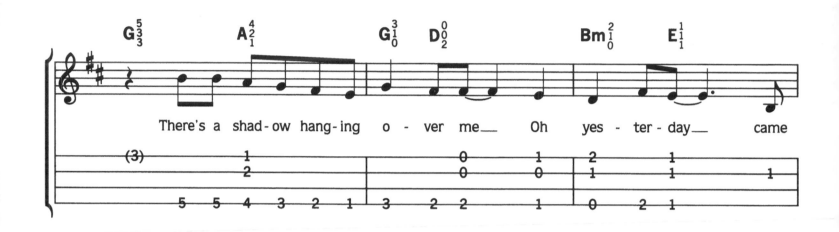

There's a shad-ow hang-ing o - ver me___ Oh yes - ter - day___ came

sud - den - ly.___ Why she had to go I don't

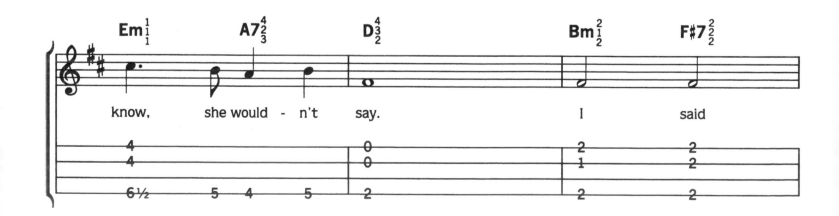

know, she would - n't say. I said

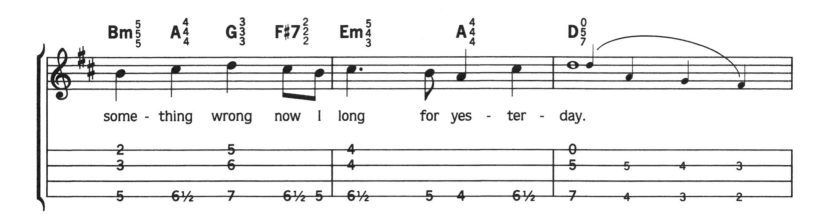

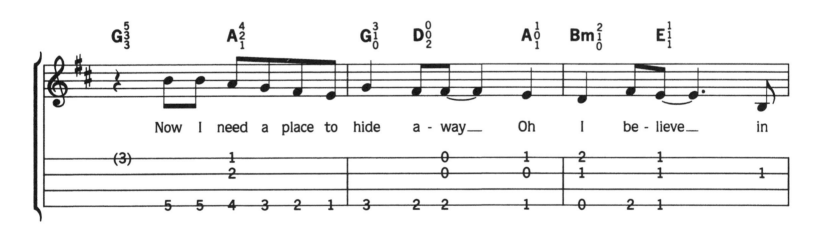

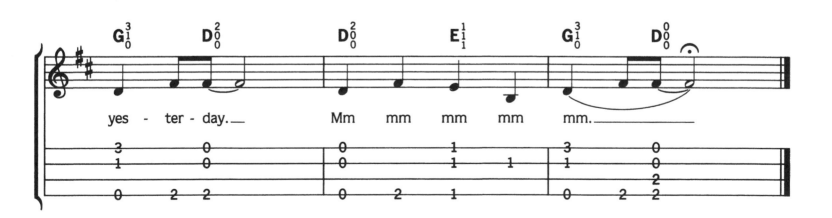

MICHELLE

The back-up chords are for a dulcimer tuned DD-A-D. Please note the tuning for Michelle is CC-F#-D.

Words and Music by JOHN LENNON
and PAUL McCARTNEY

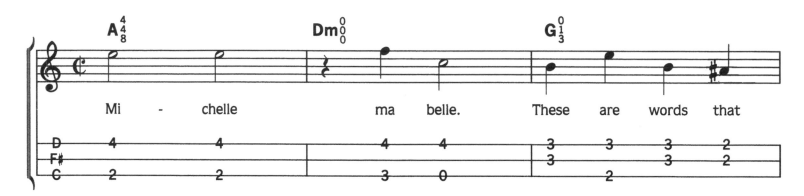

Mi - chelle ma belle. These are words that

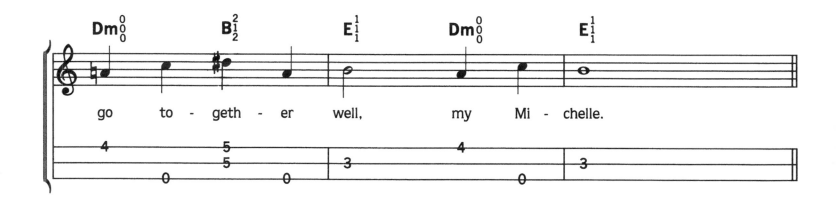

go to - geth - er well, my Mi - chelle.

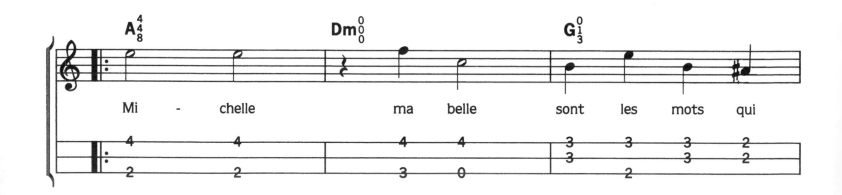

Mi - chelle ma belle sont les mots qui

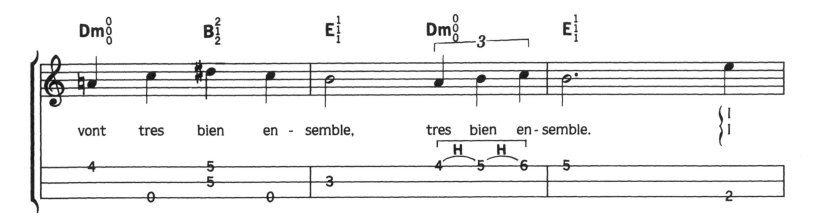

vont tres bien en-semble, tres bien en-semble.

love you, I love you, I love you,
need to, I need to, I need to.
want you, I want you, I want you.

That's all I want to
I need to make you
I think you know by

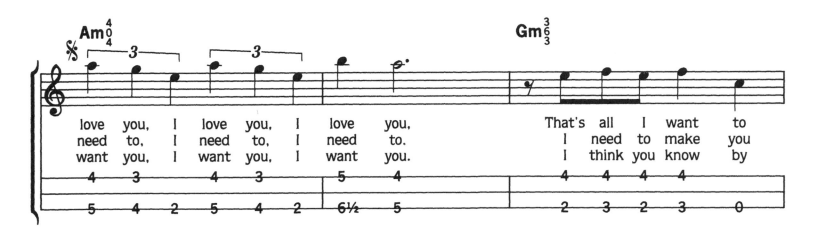

say. Un-til I find a way_____ I will Un-
see what you mean to me._____ Un-
now. I'll get to you some-how._____ Un-

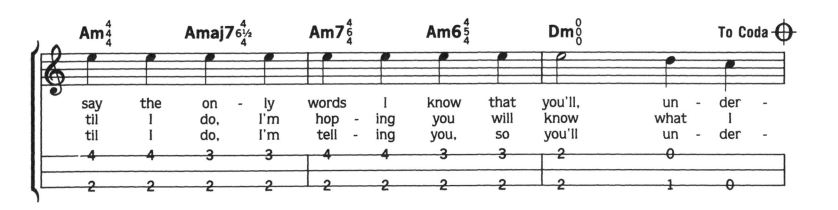

say the on-ly words I know that you'll, un-der-
til I do, I'm hop-ing you will know what I
til I do, I'm tell-ing you, so you'll un-der-

To Coda

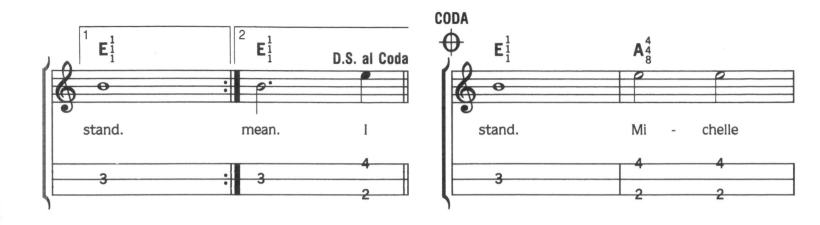

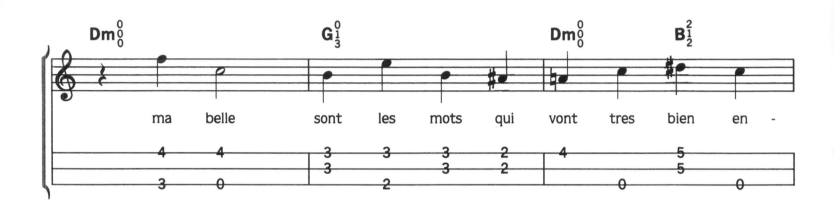

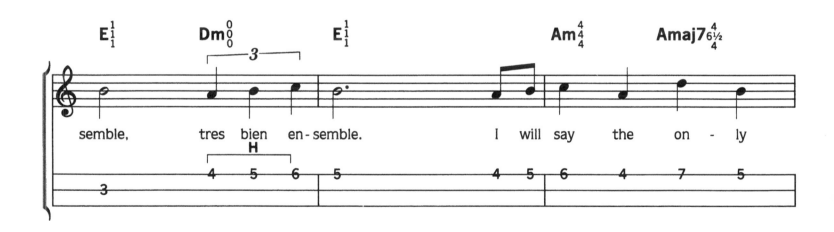

HERE COMES THE SUN

Words and Music by
GEORGE HARRISON

Here comes_ the sun,_ doo da doo doo,

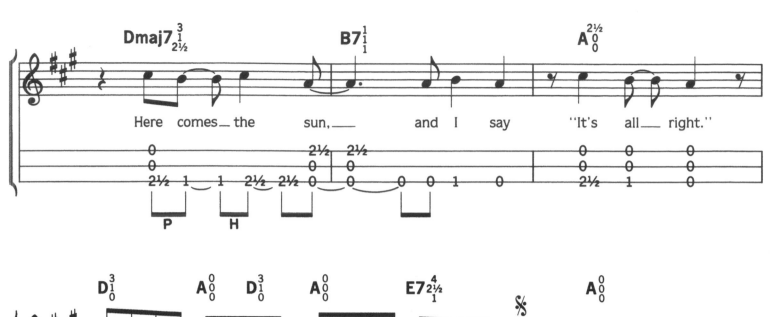

Here comes— the sun,— and I say "It's all— right."

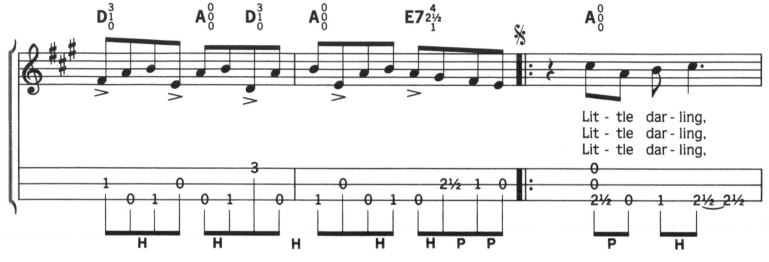

Lit - tle dar - ling,
Lit - tle dar - ling,
Lit - tle dar - ling,

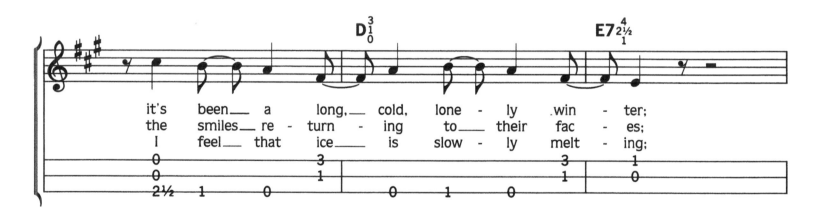

it's been— a long,— cold, lone - ly win - ter;
the smiles— re - turn - ing to— their fac - es;
I feel— that ice— is slow - ly melt - ing;

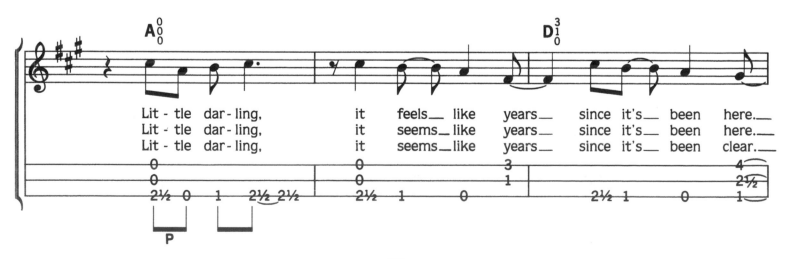

Lit - tle dar - ling, it feels— like years— since it's— been here.—
Lit - tle dar - ling, it seems— like years— since it's— been here.—
Lit - tle dar - ling, it seems— like years— since it's— been clear.—

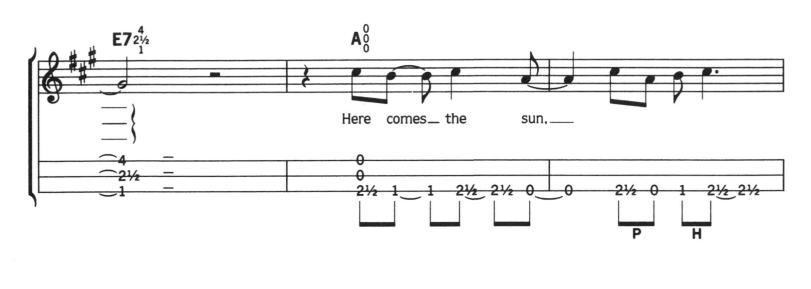

Here comes— the sun,—

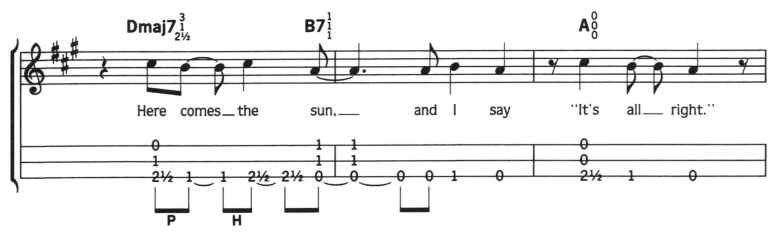

Here comes—the sun,— and I say "It's all— right."

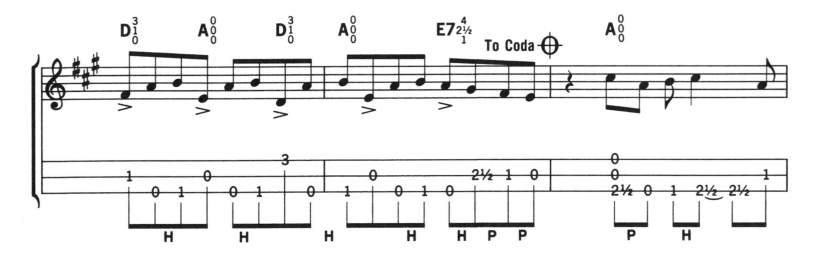

To Coda

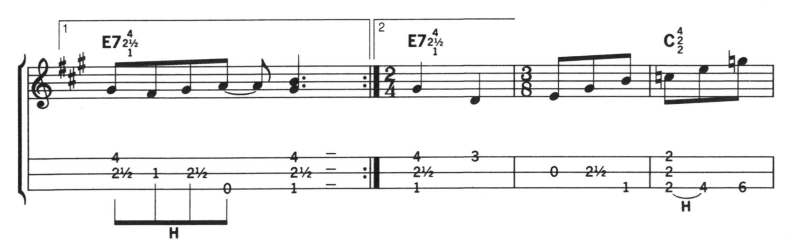

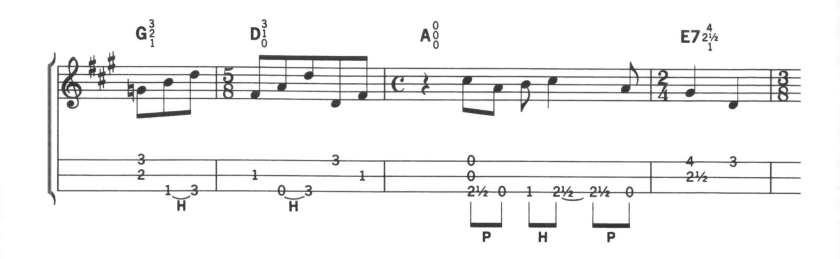

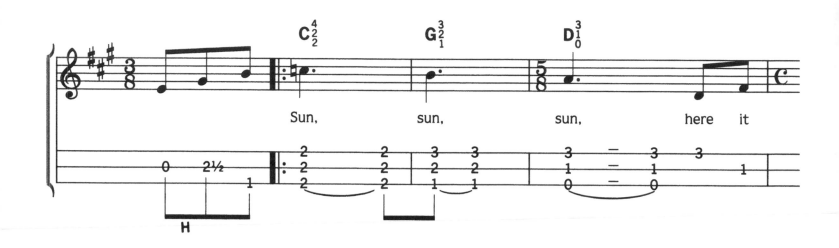

Sun,   sun,   sun,   here it

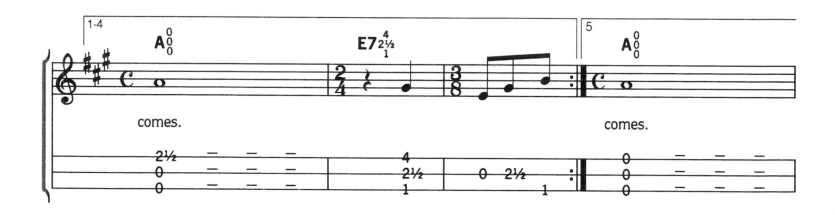

comes.   comes.

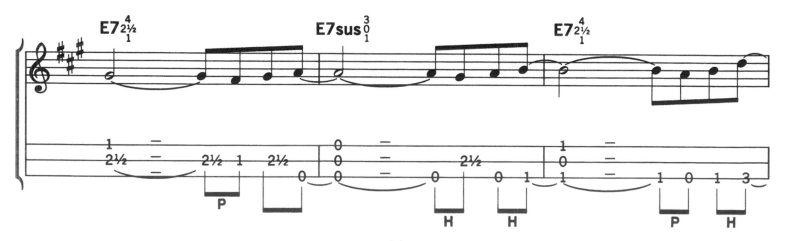

Here comes the sun,

Here comes the sun,

It's all right,

It's all right.

ADDITIONAL BACK UP CHORDS FOR:

MIXOLYDIAN MODE   DD-A-D (1-5-1)

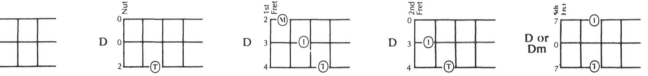

T = Thumb   M = Middle   I = Index

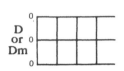
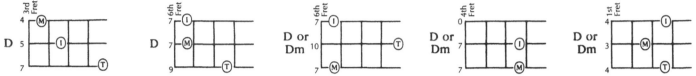
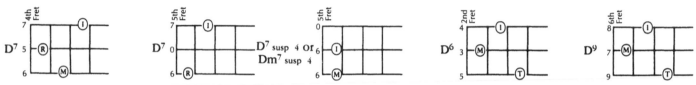
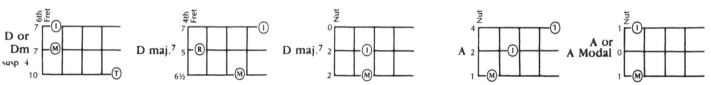
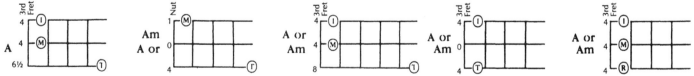
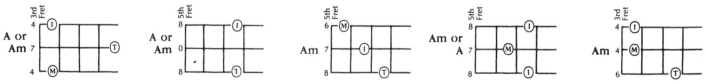
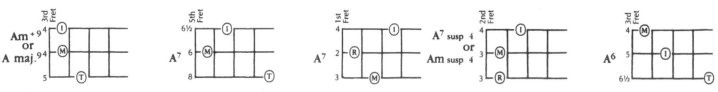

62

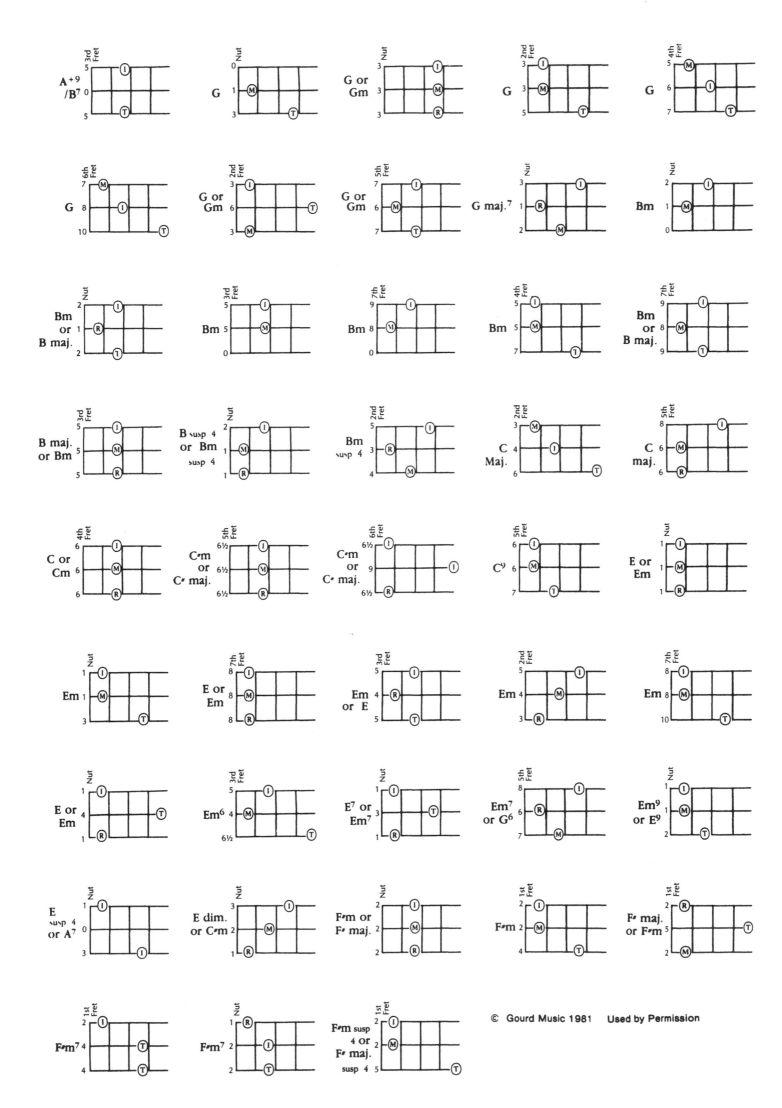